Remembrance Things Past

Ross-on-Wye
1869-1930

by Fred Druce

'When to the sessions of sweet silent thought
I summon up remembrance of things past' .....
(Shakespeare)

Published by
A. Druce
Ross-on-Wye

First impression 1988

Copyright © Fred Druce, 1988

ISBN 0 9509224 1 2

Printed in England by Orphans Press Ltd.,
Leominster, Herefordshire.

To
A. and **D.**

Also by the same author,
A Good Plain Country Town — Ross-on-Wye 1800-1930.
The Light of Other Days — Country Life Around Ross 1870-1940.

Contents

Acknowledgements

Foreword

Introduction

Perambulation	1
Market House Echoes	21
Horse and Horsepower	33
Schoolchildren	42
In The Shadows of the Church	49
Riverside	56
A Miscellany	63
Thinking Aloud	83
Bibliography	85

Acknowledgements

My most grateful thanks are due to the following:- the late Mr A. Butcher, the late Miss H. Smith, the late Mr W. Davies and the late Mrs I. Meredith for their valuable recollections of the past; the *Ross Gazette* for access to their earlier publications; Herefordshire County Records Office, and particularly to Mr E. J. C. West for reading my manuscript and for kindly writing the foreword.

I am much indebted to those who have kindly given me old family photographs and to those who have allowed me the free use of their collections:- Mrs D. Alder, Mrs S. Auty, Mr Brian Butcher, Mrs R. E. Davies, Mrs P. Dyer, Mrs J. Griffin, Miss H. Leeds, Mr P. Llewellyn, Mrs B. Maddy, Mrs F. Poston, the late Mrs G. Rowlands, the late Mrs A. Straughan, the late Miss E. Tatam, Mrs J. Thomas and Mrs K. Turner.

Ross-on-Wye.   FRED DRUCE.

Foreword

THE LAST FEW years have seen more structural development in Ross and more encroachment on the surrounding countryside than ever before. An examination of the map of c1920 reproduced with the Introduction clearly shows how great the loss has been. Yet in a less dramatic way this is a process that has been going on for very many years. In his book, *Remembrance of Things Past,* Mr Druce has unearthed some fascinating facts about the growth of the town, and with his photographs has placed on record scenes belonging to the last century and the early years of this.

I feel sure that Mr Druce's book will give great enjoyment to those who have come to love the town and to those who find pleasure in the past; and many as yet unborn will find it of great value as a source of reference.

Ross-on-Wye. E. J. C. WEST.

Introduction

Those who readily forget the past
make poor guardians for the future.

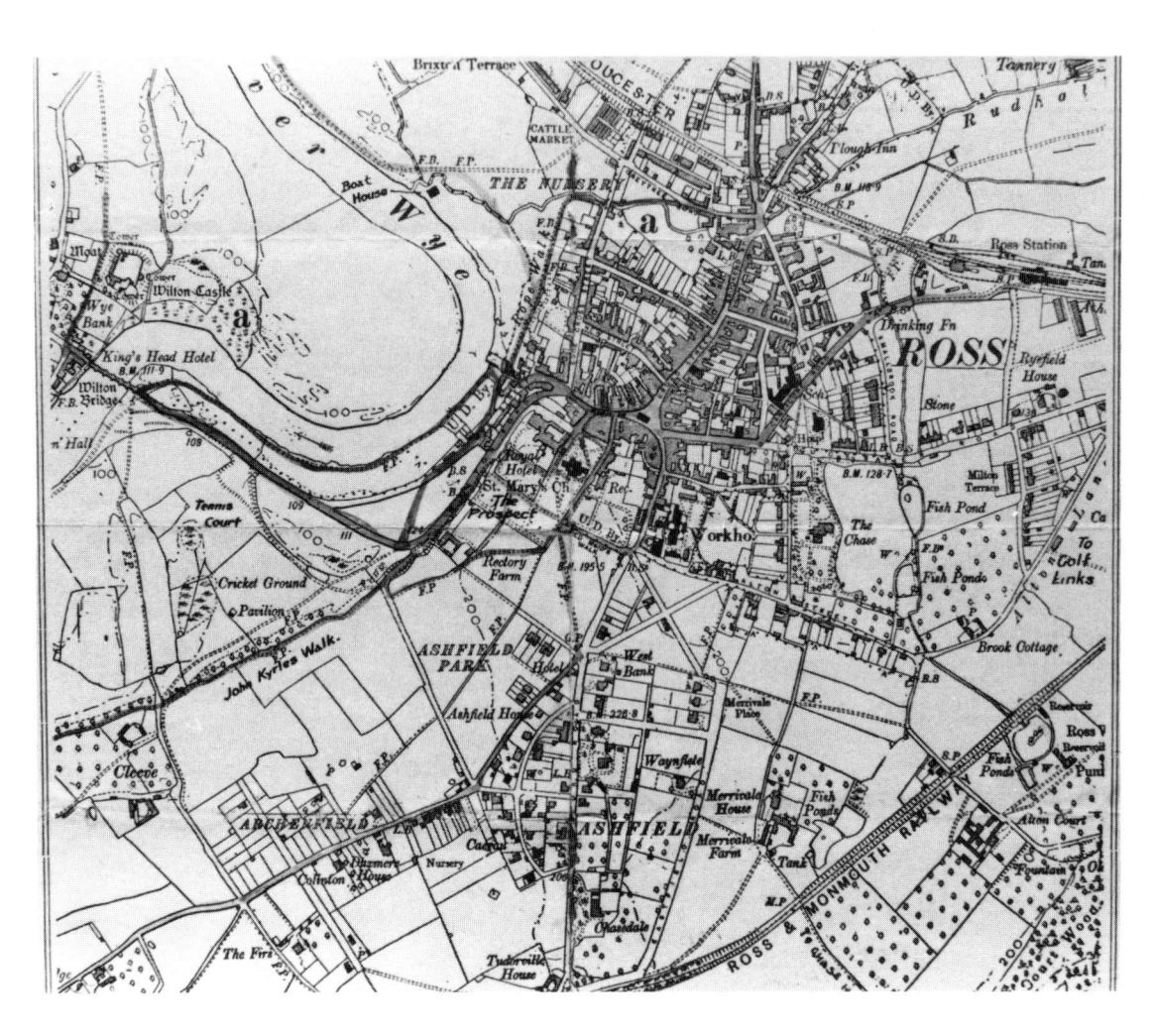

ONE PICTURE, IT is said, is worth many words. If this is so, then this is a book of words without number, for it is full of pictures — pictures of Ross from 1869 to 1930, a passage of time when, with just a few exceptions, the town had still to break free from its ancient boundaries and spill out into the meadows beyond. If this were in any doubt, then a careful examination of the map above (dating from c1920) shows clearly how close the countryside came to the town's centre at that date. The only serious threat to its rural surroundings was at Ashfield where, since the 1870s, successful businessmen and their families had migrated, building fine houses for themselves — all standing in large immaculate gardens. Encircling this island of development there was a patchwork of fields and orchards, many lined with time-worn footpaths leading in and out of the town in all directions.

Nowadays practically all are gone, fields, orchards and footpaths, lost forever beneath a sea of tightly packed houses. And if not these, then large industrial estates, especially to the south-east of the town, where at the date of the map there was a nine-hole golf course, with the bogey set at thirty-seven, subscriptions at three guineas and day tickets for 2/6d (12½p).

What of the town at that date? Visually it was much as it is now, with a population that fluctuated around 3,500, the majority claiming long associations with the town. This was also true of many of the local tradesmen whose connections with Ross were very impressive, most easily identified in the directories of that period — when sixty, seventy or even one hundred years of continuous service was not unusual (and in one outstanding example, more than two hundred years). All this is in marked contrast to present times when the movement of population and commerce is so volatile — more so in recent times and partly the reason why Ross is no longer the tightly knit community that it was at the date of the map. In almost all respects, at that time it was little more than a large village (to 'outsiders' it is probably still that now) with the open countryside no further than the corner of many of its streets.

As each year passes, the number of people contemporary with those times becomes gradually smaller, until soon all that will remain will be documents, the recorded word and old photographs such as fill this book. Together they create a picture of what must now seem like 'pipe-dream days' — days when the town grew at a sensible pace, and threatened no one. Unfortunately this is no longer so, as for better or worse it is swept along on a wave of development that many find disturbing. Increasingly, Ross is now suffering the same fate as other small towns since its destiny is determined from without rather by those who live and work here. In the opinion of many there is now a growing danger of over-development as greater demands are made on this ancient market town, renowned since the early nineteenth century as the Gateway to the Wye. At present it is a somewhat cluttered gateway, particularly to the north of the town where almost overnight acres of farmland have been buried beneath a mass of concrete and iron. Hardly the ideal things to be set at any gate, let alone at one that stands in an area of such great beauty!

Naturally, in striking a sensible balance there are many considerations to be taken into account — and even if it were desirable it would be entirely foolish to expect the town to remain forever in glorious isolation. Nowadays, this is quite impossible. And yet, if Ross is to retain its identity, there must be greater awareness of the dangers that lie ahead, especially in allowing large and irresponsible developments, or those of a highly emotive nature that benefit only those with vested interests and do little, if anything, for the long-term prospects of the town. Now more than ever there is a need for caution and sound judgement. This above all, if regrettable and lasting mistakes are to be avoided!

Finally, at the date of the map a local guide book described Ross as a 'quaint old-world town that had been richly endowed by nature and also the hand of man' — with certain reservations a justified claim at that time. However, seventy years on, times and the town have changed far beyond what anyone could have then perceived, until now it is very much open to question as to whether the 'hand of man' has in fact, got out of hand. Therefore, what now for the future of Ross? Who knows? Only time will tell.

Perambulation

AT A TIME when there is so much reconstruction taking place (though some would argue that it is destruction) it is perhaps an interesting exercise to look back awhile and with the aid of the following collection of photographs see how the town has changed since the turn of the century.

Until fairly recently, with the exception of a few areas, the overall appearance of Ross has broadly remained the same as it was in the mid-nineteenth century when many of the present buildings were erected and the older ones given a Victorian face-lift. Naturally there have been alterations, for example, new shop fronts and differing colour schemes. But in general the town still looks very much the same as it did roughly a hundred years ago.

However, at the time of writing, parts of it are about to change dramatically and the long established outline of some of the streets is about to vanish forever. This, for many, is regrettable, particularly so for those with long and happy associations with Ross. Nevertheless, no matter what our feelings may be it is impossible to resist change, for without it the town would have sunk into obscurity centuries ago.

Accepting this fact, it therefore becomes incumbent upon those in authority, especially those whose powers lie in the field of planning, to exercise their responsibilities with great care, constantly bearing in mind that their decisions, more than most, will continue to blight or enhance the town for generations to come.

Broad Street, as seen from the Market House balcony at the latter part of the last century. Although present day buildings are almost identical with those seen here the condition of the road is rather primitive with the gutters being made of rough stone sets.

This somewhat smokey photograph dates from the turn of the century and was taken from the grounds of Springfield. The ploughed field with the path running through it is Cawdor and is now fully developed, as is so much of the farming land that once nestled tight against the old boundaries of the town. Indeed, the photograph is a first class example of this, for at the time it was taken, the countryside and Ross were separated by no more than the width of a railway line, seen immediately in front of the old houses that lined the old Nursery Road.

If you look carefully, you can just make out the clock tower on the Market House, though from this angle it looks completely out of place. The two tall chimneys were demolished many years ago, but are still remembered as landmarks of the town. On the left is the old Brewery chimney and in the centre, that of the gas works, a reminder of the days when the town's supply of gas was entirely 'homemade'.

The almost complete dependence on coal fires for cooking etc. is plainly apparent by the amount of smoke pouring from many chimneys, even though it is high summer, (note the surrounding trees). Incidently, in 1912, Forest Nuts were 21/- (£1·05p) a ton delivered and best Stafford, between 22/- (£1·10p) and 24/- (£1·20p) a ton.

Judging by the number of old photographs of Ross that have survived the two most popular subjects for any photographer were first the Market House and then Broad Street, seen here on a wet day early this century.

Above the shop fronts the buildings are practically unchanged to this day and though not outstanding in any way they are nevertheless entirely compatible with one another and free from the ugly and abrasive lines that are often part of present day architecture. What has changed, and very much so, is the style of dress, the type of transport and quite obviously, from the discussion taking place in the middle of the road, the general pace of life.

Among the many taverns that were once in Broad Street there was the Saddler's Arms Inn, thought to have been the building on the left with a cross at the gable end. At one time the landlord of this inn, William Morgan, was also a collar and saddle maker. However, by 1864 this old inn had gone out of business and was described as the former Saddler's Arms. Another interesting fact about this area is that in 1790, it was known as The Knapp (small hill) and described as being near the site of the old Bell Forge. (*Ross Gazette* 1921.)

A not so busy day in Broad Street early this century when a local mongrel almost has the road to itself.

The rather ornate oil lamps on the right were not part of the local street lighting but the private property of Innell and Wharton, the ironmongers, whose shop is close by. With today's planning restrictions in mind it would be interesting to know if any form of official consent was required prior to the erection of this attractive form of 'street furniture'.

The range of Innell and Wharton's ironwork was quite extensive, as was expected in those times. Besides general hardware they also carried a comprehensive range of agricultural machinery, and if required could even supply and erect an iron barn, one of which still stands at the side of the A4137 near St. Owen's Cross.

These two scenes of Broad Street are separated by almost thirty years. The photograph above dates from about 1900, an age when the centre of the road was as safe a place for children to walk as the pavements.

Until early this century wooden barrels were made in Broad Street by the small firm of Lugg and Sons, and their cooper's yard was at the rear of some shops at the lower part of the street. When completed the barrels were stacked at the roadside to await transportation and if you look on the right-hand side you can see a load just about to depart.

In the later photograph below, the motor car had already begun to make its mark in Ross, though some years had still to pass before the town became suffocated by it, as very often happens nowadays.

Just a glance through any local business directory of the early years of this century is sufficient to appreciate how many of the daily requirements were actually made in the town by local craftsmen. A good example of an early local industry was Edmund Turner's Boot and Shoe factory that for many years was situated at the bottom of Broad Street. In the photograph above, the entire staff of twenty-four is posing with a waggon carrying the raw material for this old craft — in this case, 200 cattle hides tanned with English oak bark, valued then at nearly £500. Some idea of the range of leather goods made by this old firm can be seen from their advertisement which appeared in a Coaching Guide of 1891. Besides two shops in Ross, 'Turner's' also had outlets in Monmouth and Abergavenny, although the majority of their goods were made at the rear of the shop seen here. On a greatly reduced scale 'Turner's' continued to operate until shortly after the 1939-45 war.

"COMET" COACH.

ROSS, MONMOUTH, ABERGAVENNY.

Passengers by the above Coach are most respectfully informed that they can be supplied at either of the above Towns with

EDMUND TURNER & CO.'S

World-renowned Ladies' and Gentlemen's High-Class

BOOTS & SHOES

(TRADE-MARKED "KYRLE"),

Manufactured by themselves from the best Bark-Tanned Leather, and the Wear guaranteed.

HUNTING, FISHING, SHOOTING, AND WALKING BOOTS AND SHOES

Of every description kept in Stock, or made to order.

GOODS sold as "HANDSEWN" are warranted GENUINE all throughout.

Customers can rely upon having the same Fittings afterwards.

Yet another industry with long associations with Ross was that of Blake Brothers, General Ironmongers. This old company was established in 1815 and for many years their hardware store seen above was situated at the corner of Station Street. Their foundry, where many of the items seen here were made, was in the Crofts, the site also for another much larger foundry, that of Perkins and Bellamy whose speciality was agricultural implements. If you look above the shop front you will see a large iron kettle. This, it was said, was made especially for the festivities that followed the opening of the Gloucester, Ross and Hereford railway in 1855. Its purpose, so the story goes, was to provide tea for the children's party that followed the opening ceremony. If this was so, then the old kettle must have required filling many times for it was reported that at the party mentioned, 180 gallons of tea were drunk and 600 lbs of plum cake eaten.

CELEBRATED FAMILY ALES
Brewed from the very best Barley-Malt and Hops.

The Alton Court Brewery. Ross

Just off Broad Street, filling almost the entire length of Station Street and a good deal of Henry Street there was until 1957 the Alton Court Brewery. Although many years have passed since beer was made here the old buildings still look very much the same as they did in the late nineteenth century, the date of the engraving above. A brief account of this old company has already been dealt with in an earlier book of mine. Therefore, for a moment, let those who especially like a glass of beer, mull over the prices seen below.

LIST OF PRICES.

MILD ALES.

NO.		Per Gal.	NO.		Per Gal.
1	X Harvest Ale		4	AX	1/2
2	XX	-/10	5	AXX	1/4
3	XXX	1/-	6	AXXX	1/6

BITTER ALES.

7	Diamond Pale Ale	1/2	9	India Pale Ale	1/6
8	,, ,,	1/4	10	East India Pale Ale	1/8

STOUTS.

11	Porter	1/2	12	Stout	1/4

CELEBRATED FAMILY ALES.

13	Golden Crown	1/-	14	Golden Hop	1/2

Brookend Street and part of Broad Street, 1902, with the flags and bunting being aired to celebrate the coronation of Edward VII.

The three buildings on the right mark the beginning of Brookend Street, though nowadays only the first two remain. Those who are familiar with this part of Ross will probably be surprised to see how extensive the Barrel Inn originally was, plus the fact that it was also a brewery. In 1851, the Barrel Inn was kept by George Hall. However, by 1867, it has passed into the care of the Goulding family and there it remained until the early years of this present century probably still selling beer at their prices of 1896 when it was advertised in the following manner. 'W. H. Goulding, Barrel Inn, home brewed beer with malt hops, from 10d to 1/4d per gallon, also well aired beds'.

By 1902, the general appearance of Brookend Street had greatly improved and most of the area had finally escaped from its long-held title of being the 'Wretched End of Town'. Yet only thirty years earlier, and well within the memory of some in this photograph, this description had been completely justified, as reports in the *Ross Gazette* show when it refers to Brookend as the 'Lower part of the town being in a bad state. Something like 150 people had had notices to remove nuisances, pigsties, privies and attend to their bad drains'. The figure of 150 offenders in such a short street might seem outstanding but it should be remembered that until the early years of this century the population of Brookend Street was far greater than nowadays, with many living in a series of small terraced houses tucked away behind the main buildings. These were Clarkes Row, Townsend Row and a particularly poor group called Batts Gardens. All are now gone.

Finally, returning to the photograph, two things catch the eye; first, the little fellow with his mother's shopping bag, and next, the forlorn stance of the long-suffering horse.

Even today, after many attempts to prevent it, the sight of Brookend Street under water is not uncommon though it is doubtful if every house or shop is so well provided with gang planks as they were in this picture of the 1930s.

Except for the removal of Blakes old ironmongers shop, (today, this is the entrance to a car park) very little has changed in this part of the town. Yet only a few years ago there were several still alive who could vividly remember, where now there is a large garage, (seen on the left) cowsheds and pigsties, and behind them the small fields and orchard that were part of a farm.

Dominating the end of the street there is the town's mill and if you look closely at the small building to the right of the mill you will see an old millstone.

The sight of Langford's Dining Rooms on the right will bring back happy memories to those who can recall the tantalising smell of homemade faggots that once prevailed in this street. For many, but particularly the 'country folk' in town on market days, a meal of faggots and peas and a good cup of tea at Langford's was the highlight of the day — and when I think of those times I can still see clearly the tiny dining-rooms crowded to the point of overflowing, full of satisfied 'faggot fans'. Alas, it is no more!

Until 1830, when the boundaries were redrawn, this part of Brookend Street marked the limits of the town. Therefore, once through the tollgates that barred the roads here, the early nineteenth century traveller was immediately in the 'considerable suburbs of Brampton and Overross Streets'. (*Early Guide Book.*) And yet, only thirty-two years earlier, Bonner, in a very flowery description of this same area had spoken about 'the fields adjoining a copious stream, (the Rudhall Brook) where grazing cattle occupy the very brink of the opposite verdant level, produce an effect inconceivably charming .... the scene is still further augmented by the busy sound of an adjacent mill and dashing murmur of its cascade'. (*Ten Views of Goodrich Castle,* Bonner 1798.)

Since then, almost two centuries have passed, though in many respects history has stood still for this part of Ross, as at the time of writing there is still a mill here while the dashing cascade of the nearby stream remains a prominent though somewhat dirty feature.

Taken on a fine summer day early this century, the photograph above shows the Railway Inn to good advantage. Once called the Railway Tavern, parts of it are said to date from the seventeenth century. The building close by dates from around the same period. For half a century it was the home of Samuel Kell, described in a business directory of 1851 as Iron and Brass Founder and Machine Maker. As a matter of interest, his old workshops that stood along Millpond Street have only recently been demolished.

On the right of the picture, with the sunblinds protecting a wide variety of contents, is the Brookend Post Office and general store kept by the Williams sisters. By all accounts these ladies sold practically everything including bread and cakes baked in the bakehouse below street level (a fuller account of this shop is contained in my earlier book entitled, *A Good Plain Country Town*). Until it was burned down early this century, this old shop was the centre of the universe, or so the young children with their occasional pocket money thought.

Both of these photographs of Brookend, or Fiveways Junction as it is often called, date from early this century.

A common feature of all the early street scenes of Ross and for any other small town of this period is the natural way the centre of the road was used for both play and general discussion. If for nothing else, those traffic free days are to be envied, for without doubt the town then was a much safer place to live in.

When compared with the majority of the main streets of Ross, the Gloucester Road, seen here, is a relative newcomer having been opened little more than one hundred and sixty-two years. When first constructed it was hardly more than a wide track that ran through a series of small fields and orchards. Yet even in this primitive state it was vastly superior to the Old Gloucester Road that it had replaced.

The photograph above dates from the turn of the century. An age still untroubled by the internal combustion engine — and very little else it would seem. With no great pressure for space the centre of the road appears to have been quite adequate for traffic going in both directions leaving both sides of the road for parking with its inevitable results. And to think, that at this time this was the main road to London.

The photograph of this old Ross firm in Gloucester Road was taken in 1897, the year Queen Victoria celebrated her Diamond Jubilee, hence the decorations. At this date and for many years later James Woolf owned a small haulage and building business, beautifully advertised in the large painting on the left. The small vehicle seen here is a scaled-down version of a horse-drawn pantechnicon, or put more simply, a furniture van. At the rear of this there is a nice touch with the church spire rising behind a group of trees.

Besides general goods, Mr Woolf also hired out a variety of carriages and during the summer months ran short excursions into the Forest of Dean. The climax of those enjoyable Sunday afternoons came during the journey home when Mr Woolf, 'on top of the box', led the singing as the horse-drawn brake rumbled slowly towards Ross, 'and work next day'.

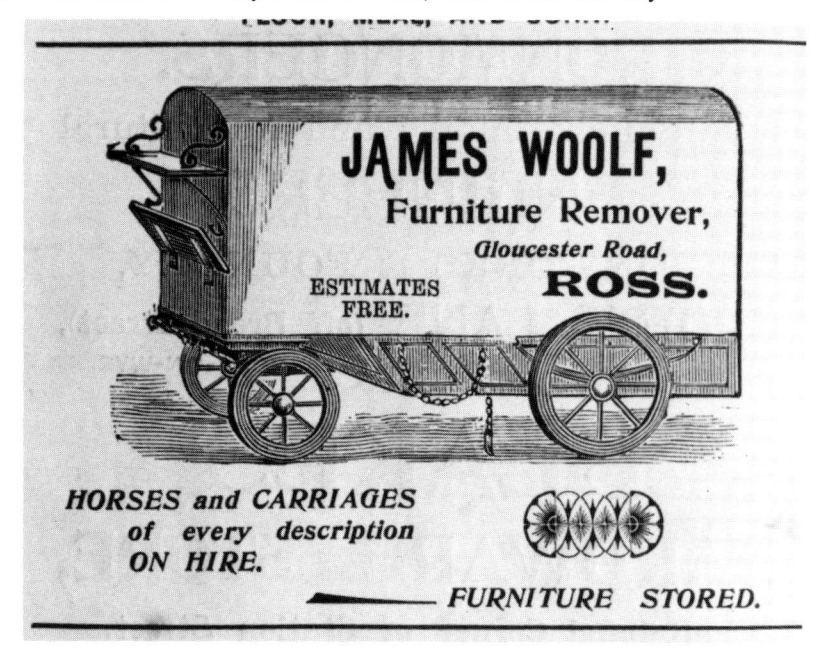

In the early nineteenth century the only public medical centre in Ross was a small dispensary in Brookend Street where the standard treatment was fairly basic. Those who required more specialised attention or had suffered serious accidents were taken to Hereford Infirmary. Later in the century the dispensary was moved to a larger building in New Street which facilitated better care. Even so, at times, there was still insufficient space to accommodate those who required treatment.

In 1879 however, following a large bequest by the vicar of Goodrich, the prospects of the local sick were greatly improved when our present hospital was opened in the Gloucester Road, seen above at the turn of the century. The large wing seen on the left of the building was for many years the operating theatre. This is no longer used as such, but in the early years of this present century this was considered to be 'one of the most unique theatres in the Province'. (*Ross Gazette*, 1910.)

Below there is an advertisement that is self-explanatory and no doubt will be of great interest to the mothers of the town, old and young.

The Ross Maternity Home
46, BROAD STREET,

HAS a large ward where six patients can be accommodated, a smaller one where the actual confinement takes place, and a private ward. The latter may be engaged by anyone bringing her own Nurse, or she may have the services of the Sister-in-Charge of the Home and the Staff Nurse, both C.M.B's.

The charge for a bed in the large ward is from 30/- a week, and includes everything, except the patient's personal washing, and the Doctor's fee, should one attend. Each patient may be attended by any Doctor she prefers; or, if the case be normal, she need not have a Doctor unless she wishes it.

The Sister-in-Charge is glad to show anyone interested over the Home at any reasonable hour, unless she should happen to be engaged with a patient.

High Street on a beautiful summer day in 1905, when the pace of life was finely balanced by the measured stride of a horse drawing its load through town.

In every detail this early photograph is a real gem. So much so, that you can almost hear the young lad yawning as he stretches in the warmth of the sun — also the steady drone of flies as they inspect the unprotected meat hanging outside the butcher's shop beyond him. And what is more there's not a car in sight! Indeed, in 1902, there were only three in town, all spluttering around on petrol at 1/- (5p) per gallon.

Except for the building on the immediate left, which has been replaced, very little has changed here, that is, above street level. As for the street scene today, well, that's another story altogether and far removed from those peaceful days of 1905!

Rush hour in Ross, early this century, with High Street completely pedestrianised, or so it would seem by the solitary figure in the centre of the road.

Except for alterations to a few of the shop fronts very little has changed in this part of the town. A few examples however, can be seen if you look first above the doorway of the ivy-clad building. There you will see the word Bank. Until it was amalgamated with Lloyds in 1918, these were the premises of the Capital and Counties Bank. Almost facing it across the street there is the old Corn Exchange opened in 1862. Nowadays, most of the building is occupied by a large car showroom, but in its heyday this was a popular meeting place for many local organisations and its large rooms put to a variety of uses. These included roller-skating, theatre productions and use as a cinema. At the rear there was a large covered hall used mainly as a poultry and butter market. Unfortunately for Ross, this was lost in a fire in the winter of 1939.

In the early years of this century the white building which stands out at the corner of Church Street was partly occupied by a dentist, Mr Boodle whose advertisement is seen below.

D. GORE BOODLE
PERSONALLY
Attends Ross every Thursday,
At 43, HIGH STREET,
From 10.30 a.m. to 6.30 p.m.

Also at Station Street, Cinderford, every Tuesday, from 12.30 to 8 p.m.

A LADY ALWAYS IN ATTENDANCE.

EXTRACTIONS FIRST HOUR FREE.
BRANCHES EVERYWHERE.

PAINLESS EXTRACTION.

Nowadays, I doubt if many spare a glance at the old Corn Exchange in High Street but from the engraving above made shortly after it opened in 1862 it is clear to see what a fine building it originally was. In fact, quite something for a town the size of Ross! The decorated arch at the left of the building led to livery stables at the rear of the King's Head Hotel, seen on the right. Until they ceased to run, this old Hotel, dating from the seventeenth century, was the headquarters in Ross for all Mail Coaches en route from London to South Wales.

The programme below gives a small flavour of the social life of Ross in 1864, held as you can see, in the Corn Exchange.

Ross Literary Institute.

PROGRAMME OF THE PENNY READINGS,

ROSS CORN EXCHANGE,

ON THURSDAY, 29TH SEPTEMBER, 1864.

CHANDOS WREN HOSKYNS, ESQ., IN THE CHAIR,

READER.	SUBJECT.	AUTHOR.
	INAUGURAL ADDRESS BY THE PRESIDENT.	
Mr. H. R. Luckes	QUEEN OF THE FETE (a long way after Tennyson).	Albert Smith.
	ROSS RIFLE BAND—"The Victoria Waltzes"—D'Albert.	
Mr. H. C. Treasure	THE LAST DAYS OF HERCULANEUM	
Mr. E. A. Hardy	THE THEOLOGIAN'S TALE	Longfellow.
Miss Trotter / E. J. Yates	DUET—"Courtship"—Gloyer.	
Mr. W. Treasure	A DORSETSHIRE POEM	Barnes,
Mr. F. Gordon	BETH GELERT	Spenser.
	ROSS RIFLE BAND—"Prince of Wales' Quick March"	
	NATIONAL ANTHEM.	

Admission—ONE PENNY, Reserved Seats, 6d.   Doors open at half-past Seven, commence at Eight.
N.B.—Tuesday, 4th October, Mr. and Mrs. Howard Paul's Entertainment.

J. W. F. Counsell, Printer, Bookseller, and Stationer, Market place, Ross.

New Street at the turn of the century, when the attention of a photographer was all that was needed to bring the daily business to an immediate halt.

Yet this quiet scene belies the fact that at one time this was one of the busiest little streets in Ross. For example, if a photographer had set up his camera on this same spot just thirty years earlier, especially on a busy market day, he would have caught this upper part of New Street full of life. In the roadway, and no doubt there are some in this photograph who could remember it well. There were numerous wooden pens full of sheep, their nervous bleating penetrating every house — likewise their strong sour smell. A fact worth taking into account when bearing in mind that at this same period, the town's sick were recuperating in the local infirmary that was close on the left!

By the close of 1871, this unhealthy practice had been brought to an end with the opening of a new stock market at the bottom of Edde Cross Street. From then onwards, the fortunes of this pleasant street fell away as many traders moved elsewhere until around the date of this photograph those that remained were small in numbers, and included two dressmakers, a dentist, a pub, baker, two lodging houses, and one of the town's principal citizens, Mr Downing, chimney sweep and town crier. There was also a blacksmith still working here. His forge was in the building on the right with the large door and signboard above.

The Prince of Wales, seen here in immaculate condition early this present century, stands at the junction of the Walford and Archenfield Roads. Compared with most other inns of Ross this particular one is quite new. The earliest reference to it that I am aware of is in a business directory of 1867 when the landlord was Thos. Hy. Counsell.

The photograph below of about the same date was taken from in front of the Prince of Wales and shows the Walford Road leading down into the town. On the left there is a magnificent line of elm trees said to have been planted by John Kyrle.

The lane at the right of the picture leads into what are now Kent and Sussex Avenues. Until houses were built here earlier this century, the ground was farmed and there are many still alive who can remember seeing corn and potatoes growing here, as well as on the playing fields at Crossfields.

If you look closely at the woman on the pavement you will notice that she is carrying an umbrella, not because it is raining, for it appears to be a beautiful day, but most certainly to protect her skin from the heat of the sun.

Market House Echoes

WITH THE EXCEPTION of the Parish Church, probably no other building in Ross is held in such affection as that of the town's Market House. To the casual observer, because of its weather-beaten and time-worn appearance, the building creates the impression of great antiquity but the disappointing fact is that it is little more than three centuries old. The exact date is not known, but most records seem to agree that it was built between 1660-1670, with the credit for its construction going to the Lady of the Manor, the Duchess of Somerset.

Records also refer to an earlier wooden building that stood on part of this site. This building, the Booth Hall, served the town primarily as a Court of Pie Powder, though further accounts suggest that during the Civil War, the Parliamentarian, Colonel Massey, held daily committee meetings here. The only surviving features of this particular building are thought to be the balcony rail which faces Broad Street and parts of the staircase.

Built of soft sandstone, the present Market House needs constant attention if only to prevent it from falling down. But the effort is thoroughly worthwhile and must be maintained, for over the years this treasure house of memories has played its part in so much of the town's history. Among other things the large room has served as a boys' school, a ballroom, a magistrates' court, the council chamber and a venue for public meetings, also the library.

Below, between the pillars of this 'quaint old oblong building' (*Early Business Directory*) the activities have usually been of a more robust nature. At one time corn was sold here, the regular stacking of bags against the central pillars was said to have been the cause of so much of the wear that they have suffered; though others were inclined to believe that the damage was more likely done by groups of 'Market House Loafers' who were forever 'propping up' the pillars.

When William Cobbett visited Ross early in the nineteenth century he noted that, 'The Market at Ross was very dull. No wheat in demand, no buyers, fowls 2/- (10p) a couple, a goose from 2/6d (12½p) to 3/- (15p), a turkey from 3/- (15p) to 3/6d (17½p)'. (*Rural Rides 1821.*)

When next you look at this building take your time and try to visualise those days, particularly the colourful traders of generations ago that have regularly jostled for space between those time-worn pillars; of the butchers with great carcases of raw meat laid out on trestles, bellowing for all to hear that they were practically giving their meat away; and not to be outdone, farmers' wives and daughters, confirming in shrill tones that everything for sale was 'fresh from the farm this day'.

Those unable to find room here would fill the apron below the Market House steps setting out their wares amongst a motley collection of doubtful characters such as quack doctors, bible thumpers and a variety of entertainers whose hilarious efforts were still remembered long after the laughter had died away.

However, the passing of time brings changes and it is unlikely that the Market House will ever play host to such exuberant times again. Yet, with luck, the old building will continue to bear witness to the changing face of Ross for many years to come.

The Market House 1869. I believe this to be the earliest known photograph of the Market House in existence. It is quite rare, yet the quality is excellent. Indeed, so clear is this print that you can actually see the smocking on the garment of the man standing in the foreground. You can also see that in his hand he is holding a stick, which suggests perhaps that he might have been a cattle drover and if so has already brought animals into market, which at that date was still held in several of the streets of the town. Yet another guide to the age of the photograph is to be seen to the right of this man for leaning against the pillar, is a man wearing the old style stove-pipe top-hat, its outline is clearly visible. This also applies to the gentleman standing in the road to the left of the building.

It is also fascinating to think that at the date this photograph was taken all those seen here would have been familiar with the daily passage of stage-coaches. For although the local railway had been opened fourteen years earlier in 1855, stage-coaches still continued to run regularly through Ross until 1873, the year the Monmouth line was opened. Finally, look at the windows of the Market House and you will see that they are all wide open, something hardly ever done these days due to the continuous noise and fumes.

Until the installation of piped water much of the town was served by public wells. At one time there were three, this one at the left-hand corner of the Market House, one in Edde Cross Street and the third in the Nursery Road.

The pump in this photograph of about 1890 is of fairly standard design, but earlier prints show that in the mid-nineteenth century the well here was situated lower down on the centre of the apron and that the actual pump was much more ornate. One small but attractive feature of the Market House is the gas lamps fitted to each corner (there were four in all). These bring to mind the wistful recollections of the late Miss H. Smith who was born in Ross in 1903, 'When Mr Drew, the lamplighter, appeared with his long staff over his shoulder the children always knew it was time to go indoors'.

For a classic example of improvisation, Ross-style, look at the stove-pipe protruding through the left-hand window. No doubt whoever fitted this was a firm believer in the old phrase that, 'necessity is the mother of invention'!

This general view of the Market House at the turn of the century appears to have been taken on a rather dull day, but the quality of the photograph is superb. As always there are points of interest that immediately catch the eye. For example, on the left there is a small group of men passing the time of day, completely at ease and under no threat from passing traffic.

To the right of the Market House there is a carrier's cart, one of many that belonged to the long established Gloucester company R.T. Smith & Co. At the date of this photograph the greater proportion of merchandise was quite naturally going by rail, but directories show that in the mid-nineteenth century, this particular company was very prominent in the district, as was also Haines and Company whose headquarters in Ross was the George Hotel that stood nearby.

Although photography was well established at the date of this photograph, the attention of a cameraman never failed to arouse the curiosity of the locals—though by the apprehensive way some are hiding in the Market House one would think that, rather than having their picture taken, they were about to be shot.

Here in greater detail is part of the previous photograph. Once again it is the group of men that first catches the eye, but look closely at the general condition of the road. On either side the gutters appear to be made of stone sets while the actual highway is of hand knapped stone from a local quarry. Until the introduction of hot tar to bind the surface, the roads were completely at the mercy of the prevailing weather. Downright messy during the winter months when the conditions were further aggravated by the regular offerings of the local equine population! During the summer months however, the situation was quite the reverse with dust finding its way into everything, so much so that the town's water cart was regularly pressed into service much to the delight of the children who, with socks and shoes tucked under their arms, would accompany it on a watery tour of the town, followed by a clip across the ear for getting wet when they eventually arrived home.

In our traffic-bedevilled age the casual approach to parking as seen here is to be envied. Even more so when you consider the present state of affairs with the town often choked with vehicles of all sizes and no longer a safe place for anyone on foot. Yet another sign of how times have changed is highlighted by the way the small handcart, fully loaded, has been left abandoned at the roadside, apparently without the slightest thought of theft while the owner was away.

At the farther end of the Market House there is the old chimney stack that for many years was part of this building — and beyond this, the current premises of local estate agents. Built in the seventeenth century this entire building was originally a large inn, though later it was split into two separate dwellings, housing on the left in this photograph, the Saracen's Head and next door, a chemist shop, Stafford's whose proprietor in 1867 was advertising for sale, 'Archenfield Sauce'.

The Market House and High Street, one dated about 1920 and the other a little later. The earlier picture above will be of interest to the keen motorist for I believe that the motor car seen here was one of the first to be owned locally—and as can be seen, there was no lack of parking space.

The later photograph below is clear of traffic except for a solitary cycle. But you will notice that the road surface is still awaiting its covering of tarmac.

A further point of interest in this photograph is the various styles of dress, particularly that of the children on the left.

If the photograph above is any guide then parking in Ross in the 1920s seems to have been simplicity itself—while there's an air of complete serenity about the way the old charabanc is resting in the midday sun. If you look closely you will see that there are no windows in this particular vehicle, something that would have made travelling uncomfortable when it was pouring with rain.

The picture below, about twenty years earlier, is part of one on a previous page and shows more clearly the carrier's cart with part of its load hanging out behind. Long after the introduction of petrol-driven machines, this type of vehicle was still very much part of the transport system and a common sight on most major roads.

As interesting and certainly much older than the nearby Market House is the one-time home of John Kyrle. The exact date of its construction is uncertain, but various accounts suggest that it was probably built in the late sixteenth century. After Kyrle's death in 1724, the old house was used as an inn that went under the name of the King's Arms Inn. In 1805, the inn closed and the building was developed into two separate business premises, occupied then by a chemist and a printer, and so it remains almost two hundred years on. Today part of it is the home of our local paper, *The Ross Gazette*. Before it moved here in 1915 this paper had known two other homes, that of 40, High Street where it was first printed in 1867 and later in a building on the corner of High Street and Church Street (now a jeweller's shop). The photograph above was taken shortly after the arrival of the *Gazette* here in 1915 following the purchase by Mr Jefferies of the old printing business of Powle, a family that had been here for almost one hundred years.

During its stay at the corner of High Street and Church Street (from 1883 until 1915) the *Ross Gazette* was printed by Stratford and Trotter whose elegant advertisement is seen above.

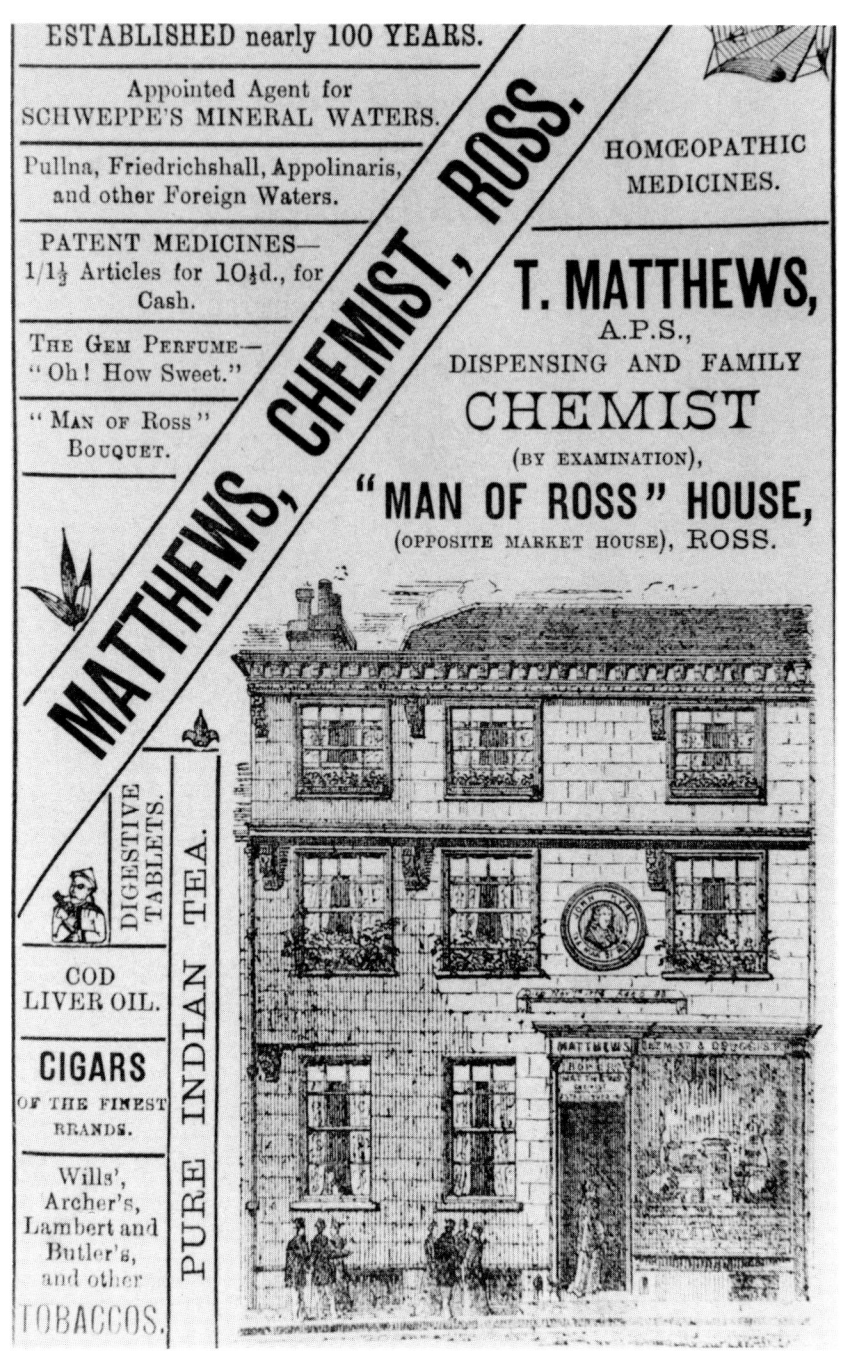

The nineteenth century practice to imitate the Georgian style of buildings ruined the appearance of many fine old timbered buildings. In Ross, hardly more so than John Kyrle's old house which in the engraving above is almost unrecognisable. Besides the items advertised here Mr Matthews also sold Chiropodine for corns at 8d (3p) a bottle and an 'excellent cough mixture' no longer on the market entitled 'Ross Cough Elixir' priced at 1/- (5p) per bottle. As a matter of interest he also removed teeth at 6d (2½p) each with the patient suffering all sorts of agony, there being no anaesthetic available.

There is so much activity in this splendid photograph that you can almost hear the different sounds as they vibrate around the Market House. Taken in the 1920s, this is a first-class example of a market day in Ross roughly sixty years ago, an age when they were still relatively unspoilt and free from much of the cheap bric-a-brac that is now part of the modern day markets.

With so much to claim their attention no one has time to bother with the cameraman who has left us with this interesting social document — something that is doubled in value when the recollections of those who were alive at that time are added. Of the sound of frightened chickens as they were roughly handled to make sure that 'they had some meat on them and were not all feathers'! Of the monotonous tones of the auctioneer as each item for sale was held up, and 'knocked down'. Of the groups of chattering women pressing and pinching the vegetables to make sure that they were 'fresh' and that they were not 'buying a load of old leaves'. And so it went on, and, as I have suggested, you can almost hear it all happening.

Away from the market, the business of the town goes quietly on and at five-past-one by the Market House clock a young stalwart is pulling a handcart along High Street, his body bent forward to help balance his load and exert the maximum leverage. Yet a sign of what lay ahead in the field of modern transport is threading its way past the Market House in the shape of what looks like a Model T Ford.

These two photographs of the lower side of the Market House have been included for no better reason than that they are 'easy on the eye'. They are also pleasant reminders of a bygone age when, as the picture above shows, there was still time to stand and stare. And what's more, even have your photograph taken, right in the middle of the road! Knowing how congested this whole area often is nowadays, take notice of the casual approach to parking in 1904, the date of both of these photographs.

In the picture below it can clearly be seen that the two women are having to gently raise their skirts in order to negotiate the Market House steps. Also of interest is the unusual design of the gas lamp.

Horse and Horsepower

I HAVE BEEN unable to establish either the date (probably early this century) or the destination of the party above but here they are, all set to go with Mr Cornelius Baynham, holding his long whip aloft for the benefit of the photographer. Until early this century, the horse-drawn brake seen here was the standard vehicle for carrying large parties. In this case the number about to be carried, including Mr Baynham, is twenty-three, a figure that was not uncommon when four horses were employed as they are here (note the traces in front of the two horses). With wooden wheels (iron bound) and seats to match, a long journey of those days was more of an endurance test rather than one of enjoyment. Yet in spite of this, good times were had and thoroughly appreciated as is evident from the following remarks. 'Parties would go for enjoyable rides in horse-drawn brakes through the Forest of Dean, we would have a picnic at the Speech House and then return during the evening singing all the way with Mr Woolf on the top of the box enjoying it as much as anyone'. (The late Miss H. Smith, born 1903.)

In those times, the vehicle above was also the regular transport for the local cricket team when they 'played away'. 'For their game at Abergavenny, (a round trip of not less than forty miles) the team left early on the day of the match allowing from three to four hours to complete the journey, much of the hilly way with the team spent walking to save the poor horses. The load was usually between twenty to thirty. After the journey buckets of water were thrown over the horses to clean them from the dust off the road. When the roads were eventually tarred it finished the horses, it was too much for them in the summer'. (The late Mrs. I. Meredith, born 1891, daughter of Mr. C. Baynham.)

The gentleman standing in the doorway of his shop is Mr George William Butcher, a Gloucestershire man who came to Ross in the 1860s. Beside him, in a girl's dress, is his son Allan, though throughout most of his life he was better known as 'Chappie'. In his early years in Ross Mr Butcher was primarily a clock and watch repairer. Later, however, he added a further string to his bow, assembling, selling and repairing bicycles. Indeed, for many years, as part of his 'after sales service' he offered cycling lessons on his private cycling track at the rear of his premises. But only to his 'better off' customers.

By the turn of the century, and in keeping with the growing interest in all things mechanised, Mr Butcher set about designing an engine that he hoped would fit into and drive the rear wheel of a bicycle. An enterprise it seems that got completely nowhere but which led on to far greater and grander things, such as the founding of the first motor garage in Ross. And, not content with this, building with fellow enthusiasts, an aeroplane in a tiny hanger that still stands to this day.

By 1906, Mr Butcher was established in his own garage in Brookend Street. Shortly after he extended his business and formed a partnership with Mr Casson, a coachbuilder whose premises were at the top of Henry Street. Together, in a building in Cantilupe Road, they turned out a wide range of motor vehicles, each one hand-built to the specific requirements of their customers. To promote their business, this small company produced an illustrated catalogue from which intending customers could make their choice from a wide selection of small to medium-sized vans. Some measure of their success can be seen in the photograph below for if you look closely you can see that this particular vehicle is bound for Kingston-on-Thames. The small group above, proudly advertising their latest creation, constituted almost the entire workforce of this local firm.

Earls Court, Ross style, with the top of Henry Street serving as the site for the local Motor Show. Taken in the 1920s, both of these photographs are of vehicles supplied by Butcher and Casson. Although this company did in fact make the bodywork for many cars I am doubtful if this was so for the three in the photograph above, all presumably being advertised as The Black Secret.

With no likelihood of police intervention, the site chosen to display the sporty two-seater below is at the top of Cantilupe Road.

Incidently, behind the wall to the left there are chicken pens. Today, this ground is covered by several small shops and the local Red and White Bus Office.

Another local man with long associations with transport was Mr S. Llewellyn seen above with his pride and joy, a 1907 Humber 10/12. At the date of this photograph the annual road tax was just 5/- (25p), petrol was around 1/6d (7½p) a gallon and to complete the picture there were no driving licences, no driving examinations and no M.O.T. Prior to the advent of motorised transport, and indeed, for many years later, Mr Llewellyn ran an extensive haulage business that depended heavily on the use of horses. During the last century when the motive power was entirely four-legged, Mr Llewellyn supplied his own feed corn and hay from fields he owned at the bottom of Cantilupe Road. These have long since been covered with buildings and tarmac.

Among the large fleet of steam-driven vehicles owned by Mr Llewellyn there were several steam-rollers one of which is seen below at work in Cantilupe Road.

Parking in Ross in the 1920s, when the Market House apron was more than sufficient to accommodate all and sundry. And that at five-past-eleven on a summer day (notice the young lady wearing a straw hat). How times have changed!

In the early years of this century, when motoring was still in its infancy, most would probably have agreed with the remarks of a local chemist who when asked his opinion of 'smart motors' was certain that 'cars were only a passing fancy'. Yet just a few years later, as is plain to see in these two photographs, the car, plus a couple of charabancs was already beginning to dominate the centre of the town, in its own small way laying down the seeds of many of our present traffic problems.

In the photograph below there is just one car and an early Midland Red bus in the complete length of Broad Street. Knowing how congested all our streets have become, one is inclined to think that, traffic wise, those were the days!

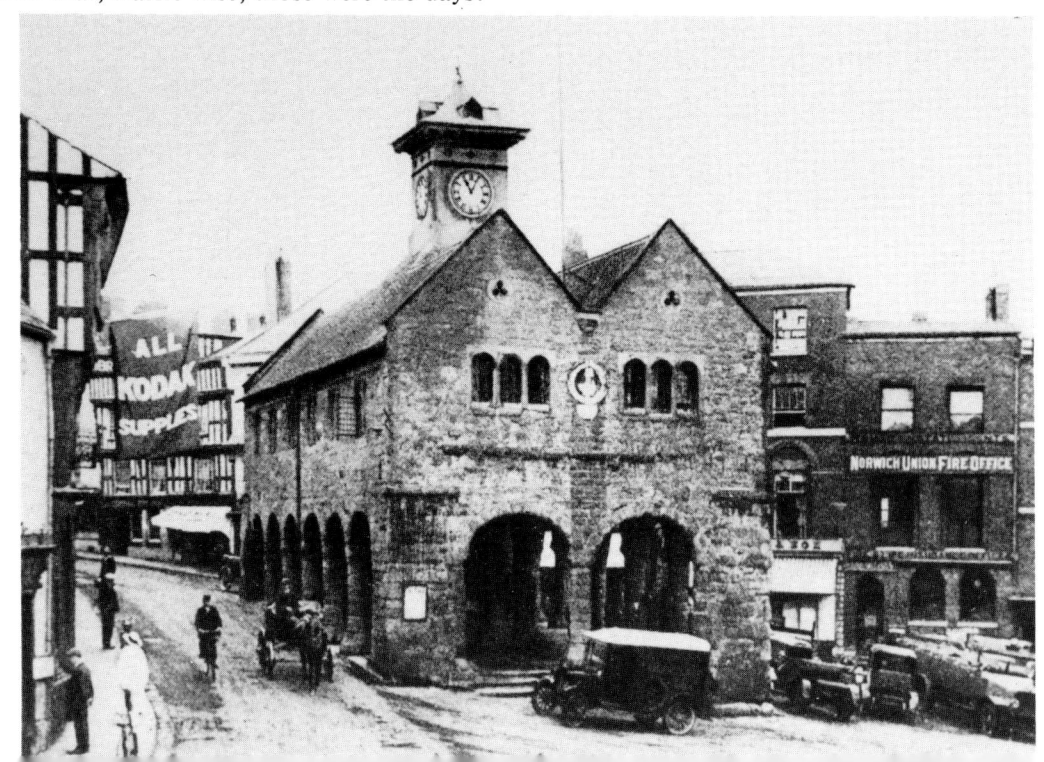

Until well after the 1939-45 war the principal coach and taxi service in town was that owned by the Baynham family. Indeed, their connections in this field spanned many years dating back to the latter part of the last century when their fleet of vehicles was entirely horse-drawn and included those with such glamorous names as a Barouche, Landau, Victoria as well as a variety of Gigs and Traps and the local Omnibus that met the trains arriving at the station.

The two photographs here are of members of that distinguished family. In the one above, taken in Wye Street early this century, there is Irene Baynham who continued to drive a taxi until late in her life. In the one below, with a motorised version of the omnibus, is her brother George, still fondly remembered by those who travelled with him.

In terms of general comfort there was little to choose between the open top charabanc above and the horse-drawn brake on a previous page. The great difference however, was its superior speed plus the fact that it never tired, though occasionally the 'brute' did break down.

The charabanc above was one of a small fleet owned by the Baynham family. With the introduction of this type of vehicle the possibilities of travel for the general public increased quite dramatically and during the summer months one of the most popular journeys for those living locally was to the Elan Valley where the photograph below was taken in the 1920s. Almost without exception, all those seen travelling here are wearing overcoats, an essential garment to have with you even on warm sunny days when the only protection against the weather was a large canvas hood seen rolled back on the vehicle above.

In the short account of Mr Butcher's early days in Ross I mentioned that he and fellow enthusiasts had built an aeroplane and that the tiny hanger in which it was constructed was still standing. The date of this enterprise was 1910, with the design for their aircraft coming from a magazine entitled *Flight*. In an earlier book of Ross I have already given a short account of this bold adventure and of the desperate attempts to get airborne. At that time the only record of this event came from the reminiscences of members of Mr Butcher's descendants. However, since then a remarkable photograph of the preparations for the actual 'take off' has come to light, and is naturally of great interest. In the enlargement below it is easy to see that the propeller is already in motion behind what looks like a three wheel bicycle upon which Mr Butcher is seated, no doubt with a certain amount of trepidation.

Schoolchildren

WHEN FIRST OPENED in 1874, the local Board School had no provisions for the infant children. These, at that date, were still being taught in a single classroom in the Old Gloucester Road. However, by 1889, the date of the photograph above, their tiny school had been closed and the youngsters installed in new classrooms attached to the main school in Cantilupe Road. At that date their numbers were approximately 186, out of a total school population of 578.

In my earlier book of Ross covering the years 1800-1930, I gave a broad outline of the academic development of the Board School throughout its early years. Unfortunately though, through lack of space, I was unable to recall the other side of school life—a side that each day, in beautiful handwriting, was recorded in the school logbooks listing subjects that were in complete contrast to those set out in the ambitious curriculum that launched this new school.

First truancy, for which this school apparently gained top marks, sharing at one time the dubious distinction of having one of the poorest attendance records throughout the country in general. The complete catalogue is too long to recall here, but the following examples, picked out at random, will no doubt give some idea of the cavalier attitude towards schooling held by many of the boys of Ross in late nineteenth century. 'April, 1886, Thursday, Bostock and Wombwells Menagerie in town this afternoon. Only 173 boys put in an appearance this afternoon'. (At this time there were 230 boys on the register.) 'April 18th 1888. Only 148 boys present this afternoon against 214 in the morning, a difference of 66 boys. This wholesale absenteeism due simply to the wedding of Miss Powers, (a teacher) which was over by a quarter to two o'clock'. An entry dated November 1889, was simplicity itself, '191 boys present this afternoon against 232 on Monday morning, a difference of 41 or half a good village school'. To continue, 'April 1890. The advent of the Great American Circus had the effect of causing the absence of 67 boys more or less. Morning muster 203, afternoon 140'. The April of 1894 was apparently a particularly good month for 'truanting'. 'April 10th. At least 40 boys less present throughout the school than yesterday. Absentees possibly attending the Point to Point races five miles or so from Ross'. 'April 20th. Only 40% of boys in attendance after two o'clock owing to Lord George Sangster's Circus in town. School closed and children sent home, the number of truants requiring punishment on Monday would have needed a machine'. And finally, still in 1894. 'Attendance shockingly low. Number of boys in attendance at the cattle market'.

Among many other revealing entries there are these. 'January 1892, Ernest Powell was punished publicly with six strokes on the hand for scratching disgraceful language on the closet wall'. 'April 1892, (obviously a good year for defiance) Thos. Davis brought to school on Wednesday morning. Upset the whole school by his ruffianly behaviour and profound language. He bit the assistant master's thumb when forcibly brought out of the yard into school. He has attended school last week once'.

An entry of April 3rd, 1894 is in a way quite touching, 'Mr. Tatam's (a master) dinner stolen by Albert Day. Day's father undertook to give the boy a sound birching. Matter investigated by Chairman of the Board'. Likewise this, for September 1890, 'I wish something could be done to prevent the infants crying in the hall, it has increased so much lately (no reason was given) as to become a positive nuisance in the girls' school'. Finally from this group there are these, 'February 1891. I have this morning admitted a girl from Hom Green, Lizzie Francis, nine years of age who does not even know her letters and who has never been in any school before'. Also in the same month, 'Admitted five girls today from Ross Workhouse, I have some seven girls from the Workhouse, they seem good children and are very clean and well behaved'.

As a matter of interest I have included an entry of 1895 that without exageration records the almost unbearable working conditions that prevailed during the February of that year but which were not uncommon in the unheated classrooms of the last century. 'February 8th, 1895. Temperature at nine o'clock only 28°, had gas lighted about ten o'clock in main room thereby raised temperature to 33° by ten thirty. At noon the thermometer only registered 42°. Two out of the three classrooms bitterly cold'. To end this brief glimpse into those illuminating logbooks I have returned once more to the subject of truancy, to an entry that clearly shows that in the October of 1922 the old Board School, now renamed the Ross Urban School, was still suffering its age-old problem. 'Many hop-picking children returned to school this morning'.

Dogged by so much truancy as the Board School so obviously was, at times it must have been almost impossible to get enough boys together to form a band let alone make any progress at a practise session. Yet here they are for all to see, the boys and masters of the Board School Fife and Drum Band taken in action c1888.

These two splendid photographs are most interesting for a variety of reasons, not least the boys' dress and headgear and the expressions on their young faces. As a matter of interest, the master on the left of the picture above is Mr Tatam who you will recall, had his dinner stolen by young Albert Day.

There was no date on the original photograph of this, the Ross Board School Football team, but I would think that it was taken about 1890. With the caption, 'The Little Champions', the photograph also stated that this team were cup winners and by their bearing, very proud of it.

For some unknown reason the majority of photographs of the pupils of this particular school seems to have been only of the boys. For a change, below are some of the girls, taken early this century during the rehearsal of a school play. Both of the girls wearing crowns are quite charming, particularly the one in the centre, who no doubt eventually became one of the leading beauties of the town.

This is Ellen, Ellen Bernard, a pupil of the Walter Scott School in 1863 when this portrait was painted. Besides here name and the date, this charming water-colour carried this short inscription, 'Festival Day, Walter Scott School'. Festival, or Founders Day was the most important date on this particular school's calendar and fell at the end of term on December 4th when the entire day was full of celebrations to commemorate Walter Scott, the great benefactor of this early Blue Coat School. The book in Ellen's hand is most certainly a bible, a small memento that each child received on their final day at this school. Except for this beautiful painting little else is known about Ellen, but I am very grateful to Mrs S. Auty, a relative for allowing me to reproduce it here.

Any words of mine would be quite inadequate to describe this enchanting picture of a Sunday School procession in Gloucester Road in 1905. Taken outside the Chase Grounds, this large gathering is comprised of all the infant classes of the Church of England Sunday School.

Just for a moment, much against their will, they have been persuaded, to stand and have yet one more photograph taken. But if you look closer along the row you will notice that there are already signs of impatience highlighted to perfection by the lad with his hand upon his hip. Look closer and you will see that some of the teachers are having a little difficulty in restraining their young charges. 'For goodness sake,' you can almost hear some saying, 'who wants their silly old photograph taken anyway,' and, 'please Miss when are we going to play our games?'

In the enlargement below, the two little girls with their beautiful sun-hats look almost like little angels as indeed did all those dear souls on that happy day in 1905.

Like the children in the previous picture those above are on their annual 'Sunday School outing', only in this case, these are the infants from the Baptist Church. For these children, the 'day out' was just the same as for those from the Church of England, the only difference being that these youngsters had had to walk a little further in order to play their games. In fact, to Hildersley Farm, where this photograph was taken early this century.

Faced with the limited possibilities of enjoyment that were open to the children of eighty years ago it would be interesting to see how the youngsters of today would react. Not very well I would imagine. But for a child at that time who knew no other, this simple day of enjoyment was something to be treasured and remembered throughout all their adult life, when in fond reflection, the sun still shone on the meadows of Hildersley Farm.

Enjoyment with no more than a pit full of sand. The photograph below was taken in the 1930s and for those not aware, this small playground was situated along the Horns road, opposite the cattle market, part of which can be seen in the background as well as the little refreshment room.

In the Shadows of the Church

SINCE THE TOWN became a 'tourist attraction' there has never been any shortage of old prints and photographs of two of its most prized possessions, the Parish Church and The Prospect, but most of the views are fairly standard. The few that are included here however, are just a little different and, as far as I am aware, not often seen.

The photograph below dates from early this century and shows the interior of the church bathed in brilliant gaslight. As a matter of interest this particular picture was part of an advertisement that appeared in a local guide book publicising the efficiency of a new type of gas burner that had recently been installed in the church. The 'Bland Burner' it was said, gave the equivalent power of eighty candles at the rate of one penny for ten hours. (About the same time the local Electricity Company were advertising that it was their product that was the safest and cheapest at seven hours for one penny.) Adding his praises, the churchwarden included the following, 'The light is brilliant and the savings beyond our expectations as the figures given me by the Ross Gas Company show a savings of £17-16-4d in the year with "Bland Burners"'. To which the manufacturers of 'Bland Burners' might well have added 'Alleluia!'

The atmosphere in the photograph above is so striking that it almost seems possible to actually overhear what is being said by the group of women framed in the bright sunlight. And what's more, perhaps hear the occasional deep sigh of the young lad to the right, no doubt thoroughly bored, knowing nothing of who died when or of what, the most likely subject of this earnest conversation.

Taken at the turn of the century, this picture captures completely the quiet serenity of those times, a precious commodity that now seems irrevocably lost amid the intrusive noise constantly present nowadays. Yet another loss to Ross has been the magnificent elm trees that for so long dominated this part of the churchyard. Tradition has it that these and others were planted by John Kyrle in the late seventeenth century with most surviving until well into this century.

The photograph below dates from about 1910, an age when the walking ways of the churchyard were illuminated by soft gaslight. The large building to the centre was the old rectory, which was demolished in the 1960s.

The caption on this particular photograph was short and to the point, just three words, 'The Prospect, Ross'. Well, it was certainly that and much more if the collection of magnificent prams is any guide. The question that arises here however is, what was in the photographer's mind when he took this picture? Was he in some way advertising, as if it were needed, that this was where the beautiful girls of Ross were to be found? Or was it no more than a pictorial suggestion to all would-be mothers that when the time came, this was the ideal spot to park the baby?

Because of its appeal I have included enlargements of parts of the previous photograph. In the first, the attractive young ladies are seen to better advantage, especially the gorgeous hats they are wearing. Also, if you look on the seat you will see a bottle of ink, while in the hand of the first girl there is a pen, and on her knee writing paper. This suggests perhaps that this girl was in service locally, and that she is probably writing a letter home to her parents.

In this enlargement the most eye-catching thing is the handsome pram on the left. Surely a child at that time could not have wished for a better start to life than a regular turn around the Prospect in this Rolls Royce of a pram. Indeed, except for an engine, it seems to have had almost everything.

At a guess I would think that the two figures in the foreground are mother and daughter, with the young girl no doubt enquiring if, during her mother's life, she could ever remember having seen the river so high. Taken from the Prospect about 1912, this photograph shows the Wye in an aggressive mood, with only the causeway to Wilton above water level.

Although considerable, the flood seen here was not so great as that of 1770, when the water reached a level that has probably never been surpassed. Writing in the *Woolhope Club Transactions* of 1870, Henry Southall, founder of the local weather observatory, recorded that in 1770, the river level was such that 'The London waggon was thrown off the causeway at Wilton Bridge near Ross'. Further entries from this source shows that during a flood of 1795, the river at one point was actually rising at the rate of six feet in half-an-hour, also that 'Ross and Monmouth bridges were said to be much damaged'. In 1831, 'the Wye', it was said, 'was higher at Ross than at any time since, and only one foot lower than in 1795. The coach was left in the old Wilton Road, and the market women brought their wares into Ross (being market day) in boats'. The final reference in these records to flooding at Ross is of 1858, and speaks of a heavy storm that Henry Southall would have well remembered, when in fifty minutes almost three inches of rain fell, 'The lower streets' he recalls, 'were three feet deep in water and the roads so washed up as to look as if newly stoned'. Which all sounds very much like Brookend Street nowadays!

An ugly feature of most burial-grounds in the last century was the practice of erecting hideous iron railings around many of the gravestones. In fact, in this photograph of about 1870 there are more about to be added to those already present. With no recorded acts of body-snatching in Ross, the most useful purpose that these particular railings served was as a deterrent to the local children who often used the churchyard as a playground, lying on the prostrate stones and playing leap-frog over the upright ones.

Riverside

WITHOUT ANY DOUBT, the greatest single asset that Ross has is its splendid position standing as it does high above one of the most beautiful rivers in the British Isles. If it were not for this, then the recent history of the town would be far less interesting, particularly the years of the nineteenth century—the period when the fame of the Wye Tour was at its height, annually drawing many visitors to Ross, certainly more than to other small towns of comparable size. To the rich, famous and others the Tour was a great attraction made more appealing by the extravagant accounts of several writers who wrote in great detail about the spectacular scenery that was to be seen from the padded seats of small boats. For the majority, this leisurely way of seeing the Wye Valley is no longer possible, except perhaps for those in small canoes that each summer drift slowly by, pale shadows of those highly organised journeys of the nineteenth century.

For many years and indeed, until shortly after the 1939-45 war, one of the most pleasant ways to spend a summer afternoon or evening, was to hire one of the many boats that were kept at the Hope and Anchor Inn. Then, in the allotted time, row over the familiar course, upstream to the boathouse, then downstream to Wilton Bridge, taking care if you were a novice to avoid the gradual pull of the rapids there.

The advertisement below dates from the early years of this century when the river trips were more adventurous, the pleasure boats still going the considerable distance to Chepstow. All the journeys shown here were one-way only. Those wishing to return to Ross did so by train while the boats were hauled back on horse-drawn waggons.

Henry Dowell & Son,

BOAT BUILDERS AND PROPRIETORS,

WYESIDE, ROSS.

Every description of Pleasure Boat, Punts, etc., Built to Order.

All kinds of BOATS FOR HIRE by the Hour, Day, Week, or Month.

PLEASURE BOATS to ALL PARTS of the RIVER WYE, conducted by experienced and careful Boatmen.

CANADIAN CANOES AND PUNTS.

PRICES OF PLEASURE BOATS.

ONE-MAN BOAT.—Goodrich, 6s.; Symonds' Yat Landing, 10s.; Symonds' Yat Station, 12s.; Monmouth 15s.; Tintern, 25s.; Chepstow, 35s.

TWO-MAN BOAT.—Goodrich, 8s.; Symonds' Yat Landing, 15s.; Symonds' Yat Station, 18s.; Monmouth, 25s.; Tintern, 45s.; Chepstow, 60s.

Telegrams—"Dowell Boats, Ross."

This interesting photograph of the riverside and upper part of Wye Street was taken about 1905. Almost immediately the eye is drawn to the old paddle steamer tied up at the water's edge. In the early years of this century few entertainments in Ross could match a trip on this magnificent vessel, especially if you were a child. For what better way was there to spend a fine summer afternoon than on a river cruise to Backney and beyond with hampers full of sandwiches and bottles of lemonade all ready for a picnic later. What indeed!

That a vessel this size once plied the local waters might come as a surprise to some but here she is for all to see, Mr Dowell's pride and joy the *Wilton Castle*. In fact, if you look immediately in front of the large funnel, you will see Mr Dowell, builder owner and operator of this much-loved river craft. (For those interested, there is a fuller account of the *Wilton Castle* in my earlier book of Ross.) In the advertisement on the previous page you will see that, besides this paddle steamer, Mr Dowell was a builder of many other types of boats. As well as this, he was also landlord of the Hope and Anchor Inn, from where he ran a lucrative wickerwork business, turning out a wide variety of goods, chairs, baskets and other such things, made in the room below the bay window. (The raw material for this enterprise came from the withy beds near Wilton Bridge.) To the left of the long boathouse there is a small hayrick with a ladder leaning against it, no doubt winter feed for the horses kept by Mr Dowell. Before the arrival of the combustion engine large quantities of hay, as seen here, were regularly kept within the town to accommodate the horses and donkeys kept by most traders for delivery purposes. This brings to mind an amusing tale of a grocer in Brookend Street early this century whose small stable and hayloft was at the rear of his premises. Unfortunately for him however, there was just the single access to them, directly through the shop. Therefore, when required for deliveries, his old donkey was led quickly through the shop with the owner following close behind carrying an old straw hat 'just in case of accidents'!

The old gentleman seated in the coracle is Sammy Jones, an old fisherman of Ross, who died in 1883, aged 93 years. In the 1870s, when the photograph above was taken, the coracle was still a familiar sight with several regularly used for fishing below the Hope and Anchor. To navigate these small craft called for considerable skill, not least perfect balance and sharp reactions. With this in mind it is worth recalling a journey made by Luke Hughes who was said to have lived at the Bear Tavern at Wilton in the eighteenth century. In just two weeks, so the story goes, Luke managed to sail one of these frail craft far out into the Bristol Channel, finally being picked up near the Lundy Isle by a man-of-war. Whether he intended to go this far was never made clear, but on his return to Ross he was received with great admiration, similar no doubt to those who nowadays sail single-handed around the world.

The photograph below, also of the 1870s, shows the riverside free from trees except for the magnificent specimen on the right, the dead trunk of which can still be seen today.

This photograph, taken in the latter part of the last century will be of great interest to many, for it is not generally known that houses once stood where now there is Blake's Gardens. For a clearer view of their positions look closely at the enlargement below, taking as a reference point the Hope and Anchor Inn to the right. (As a matter of interest this inn was mentioned by James Parry, the town's organist 1730-35, also one called The Ship.) To the left of this, rising slowly, there is quite a small village with between two trees, two rather attractive cottages. In the centre of the photograph near the riverside there is a patch of ground where Mr Dowell, the innkeeper, built and repaired rowing boats. Indeed, with the aid of a magnifying glass a boat can be seen resting on stocks with a man working behind. As already mentioned Mr Dowell made wickerwork products and on the roof of a nearby shed there are the raw materials.

After the removal of the old houses near the Hope and Anchor Inn, seen in the previous photograph, the ground was cleared and a series of terraced gardens were laid out as a memorial to Thomas Blake, a nineteenth century benefactor of Ross. The photograph above, showing the steps leading down to the river was taken about 1905, shortly after the work was completed when the steps were still a bit of a novelty. Or so it would seem!

Summer time in lower Wye Street, past and present. If as a nation we continue to misuse and destroy our surroundings at the pace we do at present, then in ninety years (the time that separates these two photographs) how much, one wonders, and of what quality will there be left for others to inherit? Faced with comparisons that these two photographs offer, some might well be inclined to believe that the future is not too encouraging, for it is a well known fact — and becoming increasingly more obvious — that left unchecked man invariably destroys much of what he originally set out to enjoy.

At first glance these two photographs are no more than a record of earlier regatta days in Ross, but a closer inspection is well worthwhile, especially of the photograph above. There, in some detail, are a few of the spectators, all with intense expressions on their faces, except for the two ladies who appear to be engaged in a serious discussion. Almost without exception all are engrossed in what is taking place on the river, including the little fellow in his smart suit partially hidden by the woman with a decorative lace collar on her dress.

A Miscellany

BECAUSE OF THE limited number of individual subjects there is no particular theme to the following group of photographs. Therefore, under the simple heading above I have assembled a variety of pictures that include important occasions such as meetings and sports, plus those of general interest.

June, 1897, with the Gloucester Road full of the procession that was just part of the day's celebrations that marked the Diamond Jubilee of Queen Victoria.

Prior to this, probably all those seen here had taken part in a service of thanksgiving held in the Prospect. In true patriotic style, this was followed by a salute fired by a company of local volunteers, seen marching on the left of the picture. Naturally, an event of this scale spanned the whole day including the consumption of an ox that had spent two days roasting in front of the Market House, and culminating in just one more procession, this time by the light of torches to a huge fire in the Tank Meadow led by the now weary Town Band.

In 1855, when the local railway was opened, the contemporary newspapers referred in great detail to the impressive way the whole town had been decorated, often singling out individual traders and giving elaborate descriptions of their various displays. Forty-two years later, during the celebrations to mark the Diamond Jubilee of Queen Victoria, they might well have given Mr Price a mention for by any standards he has done the town and his sovereign proud.

Mr Price's decorator's shop at that date was in Broad Street, or to be more precise number nine, better known today as Woolworths.

There is so much of interest in this photograph, particularly of the groups of people, that have been enlarged in order to see them in more detail. In the photograph above on the opposite page, there is Mr Price standing in the doorway of his shop looking every inch a loyal subject. The slight figure to his right was for many years one of the leading characters of Ross known by all simply as 'Rumsher'. George Richards, for that was his correct name, was amongst many other things, a cattle drover, and if you look carefully you can see that in his right hand he is carrying the tool of his trade, a stick. (There is more of this delightful character in my earlier book of Ross.)

In the photograph below, the differing styles of dress are well worth close scrutiny. Indeed, for two distinct examples of sartorial opposites look first at the gentleman wearing a cap and smoking a cigarette, then compare him with the young lad to his right 'dressed to kill' in a smart suit, leather gloves, stiff collar, necktie and in his lapel, a handsome buttonhole.

HOUSE
DECORATOR

DIAMOND JUBILEE
GEO. ROWNEY & Co'S
DRAWING PENCILS

This sombre procession in High Street, with its participants 'dressed up' in all their regalia, is comprised of the various dignitaries of Hereford, Worcester and Ross and is on its way to fields near Tudorville. The date of the photograph is 1902, and the occasion the opening of the Hereford and Worcester Agriculture Show. Earlier, in 1887, this particular event, known then simply as the Hereford Agriculture Show, had been held in fields that are now covered by several large industrial companies in Alton Road. Its early introduction to Ross was due almost entirely to the fact that at that date the town was able to offer the organisers two vital commodities, namely good roads to the site and a first class supply of pure water. Note the small child sitting on the step of a shop at the left of the photograph.

Both of these photographs were taken on the same day as that on the previous page. In the one above, taken in Broad Street, the magnificently decorated arch says it all, but a closer inspection of those on their way to the show ground is well worthwhile — in particular, the gentleman in the immediate front smartly dressed and carrying a raincoat. You can also see that his jacket is fastened very correctly by just one button. The young ladies in their beautiful dresses to the right of his head appear to be engaged in cheerful conversation, no doubt excited at the day's prospects.

In the photograph below, the procession has reached the Walford Road, almost unrecognisable with its wealth of handsome trees. Interestingly, one of the outstanding successes of the day had nothing at all to do with the actual show but with the initiative of an enterprising car owner (there was only three in town at this date) who for 6d (2½p), ferried people to the show ground.

I am unsure about the date of this photograph, or indeed, what Ross was celebrating, but whatever it was the town has certainly made a considerable effort with the decorations, particularly with the Chinese lanterns, four of which can be seen hanging from the Market House clock tower.

In the enlargement below, the small gathering can be seen in more detail. In the group of three children to the right there is a pupil from the Walter Scott School, recognisable by the tippet (small cloak) she is wearing. But without any doubt the star of this particular show is the young patriot marching with her flag, completely unaware of anything around her.

Once again, the precise date and reason for the celebrations above is not known but at a guess I would think that it was probably Empire Day. Whatever it was, the citizens of Ross have turned out in force to witness the ceremonial raising of the flag and listen to the patriotic words of Mr Southall, (the white haired gentleman standing on a box). On that wet day, (note the umbrellas) there were representatives from all public groups, including servicemen with a band. And beneath the arch on the left, there is the town's fire brigade, complete with helmets.

The enlargement below shows to better advantage some of the leading participants, also the uniform style of the ladies' headwear. But again, it is the children who are stealing the show, in this case, the brother and sister holding hands under the watchful eye of a gentleman beside them.

On average the number of processions held annually nowadays is just two, those on Carnival and Armistice days. Yet until shortly after the last war and more especially in the early years of this century, the date of this photograph, the citizens of Ross were forever on the march, or so it would seem from the many photographs that have survived.

Whatever this particular event was is not known but the rain that is obviously falling (hence the many umbrellas) has done nothing to dull the spirits of the local scout troop in the foreground. Further along the Gloucester Road there is the local Fire Brigade resplendent in full uniform and always prominent in any procession. Presumably though, always alert and ready to streak off like greyhounds should the fire bell be rung in the Market House!

Gloucester Road, full of troops in 1897, just two years before the outbreak of the Boer War. Some years ago I spent many hours talking to a Mr W. Davies who was born in Ross in 1877 and amongst his many recollections, scenes such as this were most vivid. And when looking at the photograph above it's easy to understand why. Each year several regiments made their camp at Ross and it must surely have been an impressive sight to see such large numbers of uniformed men regularly passing through the town on either route marches or Sunday Church Parades, led on the latter occasion by the regimental band and mascot.

Look at the children to the left of the picture and in particular at the 'dapper' little fellow with a walking stick.

The photograph below, taken early this century, shows the Camp Meadow alive with tents, all pitched to strict regulations. Today, much of this ground is covered by industrial buildings.

The photograph above, taken between the years 1914-1918, shows a small detachment of local troops about to leave the peace and security of their homes for the slaughterhouse of the so called 'Great War'. Look at the faces of those lined up on the station platform and you will see that, with the exception of one or two, they are all very young, with some possibly not even out of their teens. In view of all the carnage that took place, it would be interesting to know how many, or indeed, if any ever returned.

The appalling loss of life during this campaign coupled with the nation's growing disenchantment with anything military, dramatically reduced the number of parades held anywhere throughout the country in general. Therefore, ten years were to pass before the local regiment, the 1st. Battalion Herefordshire Regiment, (below) was seen in Ross again, this time ostensibly celebrating the anniversary of the attack on Cadiz in 1702.

I have included these two photographs for the benefit of the local football fans. The one above is of the Ross Town Football Club who, by the date on the football, were the cup winners for the 1920-21 season. For this team, having their photograph taken was obviuolsy a serious affair for there is not the slightest trace of a smile anywhere — and not much more among the members of the Blue Albion A.F.C. below, who were cup winners in 1925-26. Except perhaps for the gallant goalkeeper in the back row, wearing what looks like his father's cap!

Until fairly recently, one of the most enjoyable ways to spend a summer evening was to stroll down to the cricket ground near Wilton and watch, or better still, take part in the exciting knockout matches that took place there each year. For some, but especially those in the small village teams, this was the highlight of their sporting year when for just one magic evening they had a chance to play in front of a large crowd and on a pitch that was free from 'cow-pats' and had been 'mowed all over'. Sadly, and for many reasons, those days are gone and the games played there now are restricted mainly to teams from neighbouring towns still able to muster sufficient players.

The photograph above is of no village team, nor from a neighbouring town, but of the first eleven of Ross in 1910. The origins and history of the local cricket club go back many years and are comprehensively covered in the book of *Herefordshire Cricket* by Edward Anthony published in 1903. The Ross club was originally formed in 1837 and the first match was between the Married and Single. 'The spectacle', as it was called, was described as 'being a most animated one, nearly all the neighbouring families gracing the arena of play. The steady and decisive way in which several of the Married kept up their wickets against scientific bowling and fielding of their opponents drew forth repeated applause from the spectators and enabled them to win by several wickets'. The book is packed full of interesting facts and delightful 'titbits' such as this — '1839, cricket at Ross continued to flourish the while. Indeed so keen were the Men of Ross that some days prior to their first engagement they secured the services of Bentley's coaching (Henry Bentley, veteran ground bowler and coach) which evidently bore fruit, inasmuch as the plucky little club had a most successful season'. Plucky little club indeed it still is!

The most appropriate title for the photograph above, taken in the summer of 1911, is Game, Set and Match, for these are the flooded courts of the local tennis club.

At first glance, it would seem that the tennis players in the photograph below have just stepped off a train. In a way they have, only in this case the railway carriage has been off the lines for some years and has been pressed into service as the changing rooms for the Ross Tennis Club. Note the gentlemen immaculately dressed in white shirt and flannels wearing the latest in tennis headgear, a trilby hat.

The two gentlemen above, seen in apparently deep discussion, no doubt for the benefit of the photographer, are examining a roller-skate held by the one on the right. At one time roller-skating was all the fashion in town with practice sessions held at the Corn Exchange and here, in an elaborately decorated room above the Crown and Sceptre Inn. By local standards then, this particular room was considered to be quite large, and certainly big enough for what passed as professional boxing matches, though where the spectators sat once the ring was in place is anyone's guess.

In recent years the sport of ballooning has become very popular and hardly a week passes without the sight of several of these contraptions lifting gently into the sky. In the photograph above, taken in the latter part of the last century, a balloon is being prepared for flight and by strange coincidence, in a field on the corner of Smallbrook Road, (now occupied by a house) opposite the Chase Grounds where present day balloonists lift off. For a point of reference, the onlookers are standing in Gloucester Road.

Carnival day in Ross with the pavements of the Gloucester Road packed with spectators. There is so much to see in these two photographs, both taken in July 1924, that a magnifying glass is an absolute must. Particularly for the photograph below where the expressions of those on the first lorry said it for all on that happy day roughly sixty-four years ago.

In March, 1879, a football match was played in a meadow near Hildersley. A small event that nevertheless has left an indelible mark on part of the town's history for it was played under the flickering light of electricity which at that date was a great novelty, and for most their first experience of this new type of lighting. Ten years later, in 1889, Perkins and Bellamy, using their own supply, installed electric light in their large iron-foundry in Crofts Lane and thus became the first business in Ross to move forward into the 'modern age of illumination'.

For the town, the first moves to install electricity were made in 1899 when a scheme was put forward that would have involved a cost of £13,000. However, at a town meeting, this scheme was thrown out mainly on the grounds of the high cost of the installation. In the following year a more modest scheme was put forward with the planned costs not exceeding £8,000, the money to be raised by the newly-formed independent company of local businessmen. By late 1901, having received the necessary Royal assent, the installation and building contracts had been allocated and work begun. At first, the only areas in which cables were to be laid were those which embraced Edde Cross Street, High Street, Broad Street, St. Mary's Street, Copse Cross Street, Gloucester Road and Wye Street.

In the photograph above the work of laying the mains has reached High Street where the cables are being placed in wooden troughing filled with bitumen. The power base for this local enterprise was in Brookend Street where several buildings were erected to house the following: an engine-room, battery-room, offices and store-room.

Apparently the whole exercise was completed with few problems and on December 2nd 1902 the Ross Electricity Works was formally opened by a Miss Mackay of Hereford.

Finally, a small but interesting point. In the photograph the workmen are busy in front of a large shop carrying the name of Barnwell and Son. In a local guide book dating from early this century, this particular business was advertising that it had been established in Ross for more than 200 years, well before John Kyrle died in 1724. Something which in this present age of rapid change is well worth a thought!

At the time of writing, an impressive new stock market is nearing completion on the outskirts of the town. Therefore, by way of a fond farewell to a little of the town's history, I have included this photograph of the original market as it was in 1910, plus a few details of its inception in 1871. Prior to this date the majority of animals were sold as they had been for centuries, primarily at the top of Wye Street and Edde Cross Street and on 'busy days', in the uper part of New Street. Early in 1871 however, the town was visited by Dr. Thorne, one of Her Majesty's Inspectors of Health, who apparently was appalled at what he saw and immediately condemned the practice as, 'not only being behind the age but unhealthy and dirty'.

By March of the same year, following enquiries into a suitable site, Mr Brundson, a grocer and candle maker, indicated he was willing to let about two acres of land near the One Mill on the Homs Estate. At a meeting of the Town's Commissioners in early April the clerk reported that it had been agreed to take the land at the Homs at a yearly rent of £11. adding that it could be taken on trial for that period and afterwards 'purchase it or let it alone'. After one or two dissensions it was agreed to take the ground on trial for a year and permission was then given to Mr Turnock to cart cinders and clinkers to the site to lay down and form roads.

In the following months the *Ross Gazette* regularly carried reports of the progress of the new market including a joint letter from several farmers praising the 'efforts to establish that long desired object, a cattle and sheep market at Ross' and in an unusual act of generosity, adding that they 'would be happy to give £1 towards it'. Anticipating the possibilities of a lucrative sideline, Mrs Bubb, the landlady of the True Heart in Kyrle Street, also wrote to the Commissioners asking for permission to rent one end of a shed for a refreshment bar 'which' she said, 'would be of great convenience for farmers and others'.

As the site developed, the original intentions of just renting the ground appears to have been reversed, since by September, when the market was completed, the total cost for the whole project was published in the local paper. This amounted to £1,200 and included the land and all the ironwork, pens and sheds, made by Perkins and Bellamy at their ironworks in the Crofts.

On September 25th, the new cattle market was opened in great style with Mr Cadle, an auctioneer, opening the day's trading, bringing down his hammer to the accompaniment of a brass band. On that first day, so many many markets ago, 130 cattle, 741 sheep, 235 pigs and two horses were sold with fat cows fetching from between £18-£28 and sheep from between 46-63 shillings. And to end that historic day, what else but a glorious dinner held at the Swan Hotel where, after singing the National Anthem, 'ninety-five sat down to one of the best banquets it has ever been our pleasure to attend'! As a matter of interest, the report of this grand evening filled three full columns of the local paper and is far too long to include here, but on reading, it would seem that almost everyone got thoroughly tight, toasting all and sundry and singing the night away with songs such as 'The Charge of the Light Brigade', 'God Bless the Prince of Wales' and a comic song entitled 'I take Things in a Quiet Sort of Way', though anyone standing outside at the time might well have been inclined to think otherwise.

Until he died in 1961, one of the most colourful individuals to be seen at the cattle market and indeed throughout the district in general was William Lewis, better known to most as 'Cock' Lewis. Amongst his many attributes he is probably best remembered as being 'something of an expert with bees' and as a cattle drover—and it is as the latter that he is seen above. Without a doubt the last genuine 'old character' who walked the streets of Ross!

To complete this miscellany I have included this appealing old photograph kindly given to me by the late Mrs G. Rowlands (the small child on the right). On the back of the original there are these few words 'My Gran and me took up the woods' (Chase Woods). Trying to fit words to this evocative scene is probably a waste of time, except perhaps to point out that in her left hand 'Gran' is holding a bunch of wild flowers probably picked by 'Me' — and in the right, a stick, no doubt used as a support as 'Gran' carried her bundle of firewood home.

Thinking Aloud

High Street at the turn of the century.

WAS ROSS EVER like this? Was it ever so peaceful? And did old men really have time to pause in the roadway to light their pipe, head bent low, cheeks drawn tight? Did they? And was ever the road to London like this, so quiet that patient horses could drowse in the midday sun, troubled only by tiresome flies and the creaking of withy baskets restless in the heat of the day? Was it really like this? Was Ross ever like this? Or was it all a dream? It is, now!

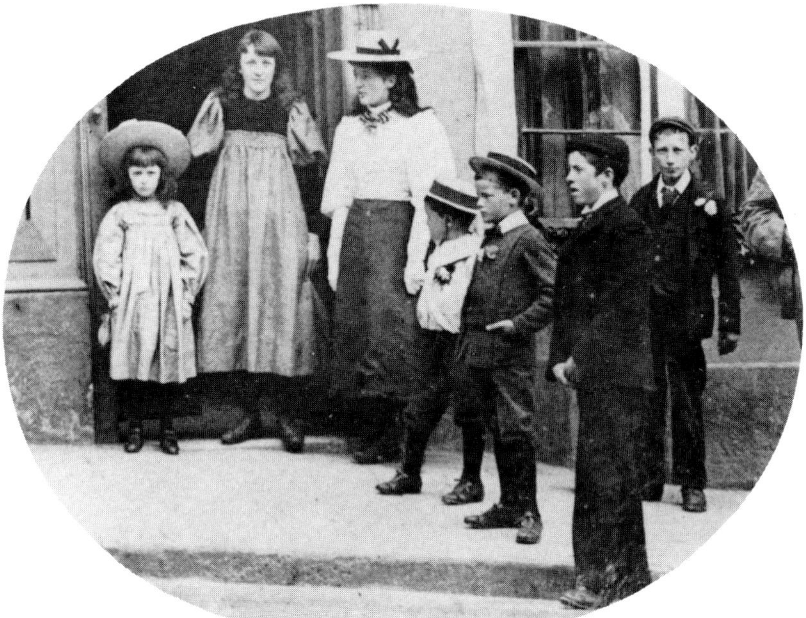

BIBLIOGRAPHY

Edward Anthony, *Book of Herefordshire Cricket,* 1903.
Bonner, *Ten Views of Goodrich Castle,* 1798.
William Cobbett, *Rural Rides,* 1821.
J. Parry, *Memories of James Parry,* 1735.
Ross Guide Book, 1827.
The Woolhope Club Transactions for 1870.

Directories:
    Littlebury, 1876.
    Jakeman and Carver, 1890, 1902.

Newspapers:
    The Ross and Archenfield Gazette.
    The Ross Gazette.